# The Pride Of Life

### All That Glitters... Isn't Gold.

# Sonya T. Anderson

# The *Pride* of Life

© 10/19/2006, 5/1/2019 Sonya T. Anderson
Millmont, PA 17845
www.SonyaTAnderson.com

ISBN: 978-0-6151-5235-6

Bible quotations are taken from The Scriptures copyright 2004 published by The Institute for Scripture Research. http://isr-messianic.org

# Table of Contents

**Part One: Ambition**

**Part Two: Pride**

**Part Three: Sanctification**

*Part One*

# Ambition

"Do not love the world nor that which is in the world. If anyone loves the world, the love of the Father is not in him. Because all that is in the world - the lust of the flesh, the lust of the eyes, and the pride of life - is not of the Father but is of the world." (1 John / Yohanan 2:15-16)

# *Chapter One: Conceit*

Have you fallen victim to the spiritual facelift? Does your personality change like a chameleon depending on your situation and circumstance?  Before we begin I'd like to challenge you with a simple exercise. Grab a pen and a piece of paper and let's get started. This list is about you, your accomplishments, and things that make you feel like you've done something amazing with your life. Write a list of things that make you feel good about yourself.

## My Greatest Accomplishments in Life

1. _____

2._____

3. _____

4. _____

5. _____

6. _____

7. _____

8. _____

9. _____

10._____

11. _____

12. _____

13. _____

14. _____

15. _____

16. _____

17. _____

18. _____

19. _____

I've done this exercise. Father asked me to write it all down. I began to write, and write, and write. I could feel my esteem build with each stroke of the pen. When He analyzed the list, I failed miserably. The things I'd were written were wonderful accomplishments. Even still, the overall list was very sad indeed.

What is the very first thing that you wrote down? That one thing is what you feel most proud about. It is what you believe validates who you are. Second, look at the very last thing you put down (presuming that you've stopped writing). That is the thing of least importance to you.

The very first thing I wrote was, "author of nine books." It sounds like a great accomplishment, but when I looked at the last thing on my list I knew what Father was leading me to see. The very last thing on my list was "maintains a good relationship with my children - a good mom." Let's analyze your list. Do you see things from a different perspective now?

Consider the one thing you believe forms who you are and who you will become. If that was gone, would you feel like a failure? Conceit is defined as "a favorable or unduly high opinion of one's own worth or abilities." As children of the King of Kings, we should certainly have a healthy opinion of our own worth. However, that should be balanced with the knowledge that our worth is nothing without our Heavenly Father.

It is very easy to harbor conceit within your heart, especially when the world views your accomplishments as a great success. After all, is it terribly wrong to have a favorable opinion of your great successes? From the world's perspective - no it is not wrong. From the perspective of Yahweh's Word, it is extremely wrong, and crippling to your relationship with the Father.

We all struggle, or have struggled with this issue. Consider what Father had to say to us in James chapter 4.

"But He gives greater favor; because of this He says, 'Elohim resists the proud, but gives favor to the humble.' So, then subject yourselves to Elohim. Resist the devil, and he shall flee from you.

Draw near to Elohim and He shall draw near to you. Cleanse hands, sinners, and cleanse the hearts, you double minded!

Lament and mourn, and weep! Let your laughter be turned to mourning and your joy to dejection.
Humble yourselves in the sight of the Master and He shall lift you up.

Brothers, do not speak against one another. He that speaks against a brother and judges his brother speaks against Torah and judges Torah, and if you judge Torah, you are not a doer of Torah but a judge.

There is one Lawgiver and Judge, who is able to save and to destroy. Who are you to judge another?
Come now, you who say, 'Today or tomorrow, let us go to such and such a city and spend a year there, and trade, and make a profit,' when you do not know of tomorrow. For what is your life? For it is a vapor that appears for a little, then disappears instead of your saying, 'If the Master desires, we shall live and do this or that.'
Now, you boast in your proud speeches. All such boasting

is wicked.

To him, then, who knows to do good and does not do it, to him it is sin." (James 4:6-17)

This passage is a progression of the pride of life, beginning with instructions on purging ourselves from this sin, and leading into how it takes over our life.

Clearly, Yahweh is not pleased with pride. It states that He resists the proud. To resist, according to the standard dictionary, means, "to stand firmly against" and "to keep from enjoying or giving in to." This word in the Greek is "Antitassomai" which means "to do battle against." Setting yourself up to do battle against Yahweh is not a good thing.

With such dire repercussions, we should avoid pride and embrace humility. Before we can do that, we must recognize it in seed form, James chapter four help us to do that, beginning with verse eleven.

Verse eleven admonishes us to not speak against the brethren because if you do, you set yourself up as a judge of the Torah instead of a doer of the Torah. It's easy to say

---

"don't talk against one another," and leave it at that. However, there are times when we seemingly have very valid reasons to speak against a brother or sister. Even if they are in the wrong, we should cover our brethren in love, and shelter them with prayer. When you expose the faults of another, you are simultaneously exposing your faults as well. The consequences of exposing the shame of your brethren is not worth the temporary venting of emotions you may experience in the process. Look at what happened to Ham, Noah's son.

"And the sons of Noah who went out the ark were Shem and Ham and Yepheth, and Ham was the father of Kenaan.

These three were the sons of Noah, and all the earth was overspread from them. Noah, a man of the soil, began and planted a vineyard and he drank of the wine and was drunk, and became uncovered in his tent.

Ham, the father of Kenaan, saw the nakedness of his father, and told his two brothers outside. So, Shem and

Yepheth took a garment, laid it on both their shoulders, and went backward and covered the nakedness of their father, but their faces were turned away, and they did not see their father's nakedness.

Noah awoke from his wine and he knew what his younger son had done to him, and he said, "Cursed is Kenaan, let him become a servant of servants to his brothers," and he said, "blessed be Yahweh, the Elohim of Shem, and let Kenaan become his servant. Let Elohim enlarge Yepheth, and let him dwell in the tents of Shem. And let Kenaan become his servant." (Genesis / Bereshith 9:18-27)

Right away, we can see that Ham was struggling with some issues of the flesh. As soon as he saw the state his father was in, he ran outside to spread the news. He was a talebearer of secrets, a gossip and a mocker. His brothers didn't even bother to look and see if what Ham said was true. They took a sheet and *walked in backwards*, therefore covering their father's shame. They didn't give him the satisfaction of joining in with his mockery.

As a result, Kenaan was cursed. Several times Kenaan is referred to as Ham's son. The curse entirely skipped over Ham and landed upon his son! This must have been devastating to Ham as it would be to any one of us today. A child is the fruit of love and was often dedicated to the Father. This illustrates what happens in the spirit when we seek to expose the faults of our brethren. Our fruit and offerings before Yahweh is cursed, crippled, and reduced to slavery and bondage.

We feel better about ourselves when we zero in on the faults of others. The more we point out their flaws, the greater we become in our own eyes. Constant finger pointers tend to have a very low self-image. In doing this, we automatically set ourselves outside of Yahweh's law. It doesn't seem like this sin would lead to pride at first, but as time goes on, the seed germinates and grows beyond belief. Therefore, in admonishing us against the pride of life, James began with not speaking against the brethren.

**Boasting About Tomorrow**

It is easy to do it. You tell someone that you'll meet them tomorrow at a specific place and time. You plan a wonderful vacation that you tell all your friends about it. Not once do you say, "if Yahweh is willing." Why would you say that? It isn't often heard. When we boast about tomorrow, we are assuming that our plans are in the Father's will. If we never ask Him, we'll never know for sure. Even simple things like planning a weekend camping need to have Yahweh's approval.

The illustration used in verse thirteen references the boasters planning a business venture. They were going to spend a year in a foreign city to trade at a profit. Sounds like a good plan to me. However, Father clearly warns that ambitious undertakings such as these must be in His will and not born out of our selfish desires.

Sometimes we make plans based on what *we* want to do, when *we* want to do it. Often times these very plans are an abomination to the Father because it transgresses His will for our lives. As a result, we suffer negative consequences while ignorant to the cause.

Be wholly submitted to the Father by including Him in your daily decisions. To think yourself as so independent that you can make decisions without Him, is an error.

## Conceit, Conviction, Contentment ~ Joseph's Story

Joseph was seventeen years old when things seemingly began to fall apart for him. Genesis 37 details the beginning of his downfall and future uprising. After spending a day feeding the flock with his brothers, he returned home to bring an evil report against them to his father. The report might have been true, but he failed to cover his brothers in love.

He suffered heavily from conceit. Joseph was his father's treasure and he knew it. Israel made no secret of his love for this child of his old age. He even made him a

___

special robe of many colors provoking all his brothers to envy.

The Book of Jasher Chapter XLI:6 -7 give us greater insight to Joseph's character at this time.

"And when Joseph saw the strength of his brethren, and their greatness, he praised them and extolled them, but he ranked himself greater than them and extolled himself above them; and Jacob, his father, also loved him more than any of his sons, for he was a son of his old age, and through his love toward him, he made him a coat of many colors.

And when Joseph saw that his father loved him more than his brethren he continued to exalt himself above his brethren, and he brought unto his father evil reports concerning them."

When Yahweh decided to reveal prophecies through dreams to Joseph, Joseph simply couldn't contain himself. Immediately he ran and told his brothers. The result? They

---

hated him even more. (Genesis 37:5-6) Later, he recounted a similar second dream to brothers and his father who gently rebuked him.

Joseph's brothers became so enraged with envy that they sold him into slavery. While enslaved in Egypt, Yahweh was with him, and caused him to prosper. However, when his master's wife repeatedly tried to seduce him, and later lied regarding his conduct. Consequently, Joseph was sentenced to prison.

With nowhere to turn, and no one to depend on, Joseph's only choice was to rely on Yahweh for deliverance. When it seemed as if deliverance was on the horizon, Joseph jumped at the chance. There were two men; a baker, and a cupbearer, who were thrown into the prison alongside Joseph. Both of them had dreams which they could not interpret. Father gave Joseph the interpretation of the dreams and Joseph recounted the meaning, as soon as Joseph realized that one of the men would be set free he made this plea.

"But remember me when it is well with you and please show kindness to me, and mention me to Pharaoh and get me out of this house. For truly I was stolen away from the land of the Hebrews. And also I have done naught that they should put me into the dungeon." (Bereshith / Genesis 40:15)

Yahweh blessed Joseph with the interpretation of the dream and Joseph sought to seize the opportunity for his own personal gain. The book of Jasher recounts this story as well and enlightens us as to why Joseph remained in prison even after the cupbearer was released.

"And the butler, to whom Joseph had interpreted his dream, forgot Joseph, and did not mention him to the king as he had promised. Lor this thing was from the Lord (Yahweh) in order to punish Joseph because he had trusted in man. Joseph remained in the prison house two years until he had completed twelve years." (Jasher XLVI:19-20)

---

When Joseph was finally released from prison, Yahweh elevated him to a great place of honor. His rank was second only to the Pharaoh, making him one of the most powerful men in Egypt. The book of Jasher recounts Joseph's words at this time of promotion.

"And Joseph upon his horse lifted up his eyes to heaven, and called out and said, He raiseth the poor man from the dust, He lifteth up the needy from the dunghill. O Lord of Hosts, happy is the man who trusteth in thee." (Jasher XLIX: 30)

Joseph had finally learned to trust wholly in the Father. Unfortunately, he had to learn the hard way. With his father and brothers restored to him, Joseph was finally content.

**When Conceit Is All You Have**

Joseph basked in his father's love. He took that love and amplified it above everything else. It made him feel wonderful about himself, to the point of scorning his brothers. In the end, it led to conceit. However, some people may adapt conceit as an attempt to recover self-esteem after a traumatic event.

The world encourages fostering self-worth, independently from Yahweh. It is harder to let go of conceit adapted as a coping mechanism for abuse. The connection between the need to feel worthy and the voice of the oppressor has the potential to keep a person bound. It may be hard to separate the two.

When conceit is born out of self-preservation, it creates a complicated dynamic. The first step toward healing begins with forgiving your oppressors. Those who hurt you need to be forgiven so that you can move on. You may have to verbally proclaim who Yahweh says you are.

Even with that said, don't expect for things to break in your life immediately. Conceit birthed out of oppression has deep roots.

The next step is to replace negative thoughts and feelings. Replace them with what your heavenly Father thinks and feels about you. This way, when you let go of your opinion of yourself, you will pick up Yahweh's opinion of you. Go through the Scriptures prayerfully and write down verses that build your self-worth the right way. Your Father in heaven thinks more highly of you than you realize.

# *Chapter Two: All That I Am*

"For you were bought with a price, therefore esteem Elohim in your body and in your spirit, which are of Elohim." (1 Cor. 6:20)

Have you ever had a dream, vision, or a goal for your life and eagerly pursued it only to discover that your plan was not what Yahweh's plan? It can be a heart wrenching experience. Once, while in worship service, a young lady stood up to share her testimony regarding going to college. She started out strong and confident. She enjoyed meeting new people and was having a wonderful experience, only to be met with these words during prayer, "I don't want you there." Father told her to leave her dream in pursuit of Him. She was in tears by this point, sobbing and wondering why He would ask her to give up her dream. In total faith, she left college and began working.

I pondered her testimony for a while and realized that we set our children up for this type of rude awakening all of the time. How often have you asked your child, "what do you want to be when you grow up?" This instantly puts them into the mindset that they are in charge of their destiny, and that they can shape their own lives. This is the world's way of thinking. I now ask my children, "What does Yahweh want you to do when you grow up?" I have since received some very interesting answers.

If you grow up knowing that your purpose on earth is to fulfill Yahweh's plan for your life, it is not hard as an adult to walk in your calling. However, if you were encouraged to pursue your dreams, like most of us, it may be hard to give up what you poured your life into and pick up a foreign idea.

When I began to truly listen to what Father asked of me, one of my first comments was, "but I wanted to..." Immediately, I was reminded of this scripture, "your life is not your own, you were bought with a price." Consequently, I didn't have much of a say in what I should do with it. That was extremely upsetting to hear!

Once you commit to laying down your agenda and picking up the Father's plan for your life you, determine to be wholly committed.

**When Curve-balls Come Your Way**

Let's say you've got it all figured out. You know what Father wants of you, and you are on the road to fulfilling your destiny. How would you react if an unexpected turn of events came into play? Let me tell you how I reacted. I was mad!

The dictionary definition of a curve-ball is two fold.

When referring to baseball, a curveball is a pitch that veers in the opposite direction from which you threw it. In slang form, it is an unexpected event, or a deceptive trick.

If a relative of yours did something unpleasantly unexpected, would you tell them of your displeasure? Certainly, you would! Do you know that we have that kind of relationship with our heavenly Father? My relationship with Yahweh is such that I have had to really 'discuss' with Him how upset I was by certain unexpected turn of events.

You see, I had it all mapped out for the next five years. Literally, it was written on paper what He wanted me to do. These were revelations I received through prayer and knew that it was from the Father. However, what I didn't know, was that it was incomplete. Two years into walking out my five-year plan, I was on schedule, doing what He asked me to do when He asked me to do it. It wasn't easy, but it was so worth it as the fruit of my labor was extremely evident. Then, the curve-ball was thrown. Nowhere in this five-year plan did it include this outrageous thing He was asking me to do.

It was crazy. I felt I didn't have the space, or the heart to do so, not to mention the time. I was happily raising my four children and progressing with what He had asked of me. However, this new assignment just wasn't in the five year plan that I *know* He gave me. You might be laughing right now but it was so serious to me at the time. It was important to me that I fulfill the call He gave me and I was. I had no idea I was missing pieces to the puzzle.

One day I got down on my knees to answer the question He continuously posed to me "Why is this so hard for you?" He constantly asked.

First, I said "Well, I don't want to make any more mistakes." This was true. I had made plenty of mistakes while trying to walk out this plan.  Even with that answer, He kept prodding and asking why this was so hard for me to accept. Then one evening the dam burst and boy did I feel relieved but not until I fully vented how I felt. My first sentence ... "I'm mad."

I was perfectly calm knowing that I can express to

my Father exactly how I felt and He would love me
anyway. Besides, He already knew what was in my heart.
He knew I was angry long before I did. I was confessing
this more to myself than to Him.

Once you discover your purpose, remember that He
gives us what we can handle. You may not have the
complete picture. Walk out His calling step-by-step. Do not
ever think you have it all figured out, you never will, and is
takes a lot of arrogance and pride to assume to know
exactly what tomorrow might bring. Keep it simple, and
commit your works to Him. All of who you are belongs to
Yahweh. Remember that.

# Chapter Three: Working For the Father

Yahshua said to them, "My food is to do the will of my Father, and accomplish His work." (John 4:34)

What is really sustaining you? Are you thriving off of worldly successes, or are you nourished by accomplishing the will of the Father? Worldly successes can easily become a driving force. They boost self-esteem. Others notice, and applaud your efforts. An entire life may be poured into vain pursuits before a person fully realizes it.

Yahweh's work yields no such attention. In fact, many will shun, mock, and hate you because of it. The world will not understand, neither will it encourage you to continue on the narrow path. You must stand firm knowing that you will be rewarded by the Father Himself and that reward is worth far more than what the world could ever offer you.

A friend of mine decided to adopt two children from the foster care system. She specifically looked for children who had severe disabilities. Both children she adopted are in wheelchairs and have major health concerns. Neither can eat without a feeding tube which needed to be administered every four hours. When she took these children to the doctor, she was asked if she knew that "these were the kind of children she was getting." Her response was, "These are the kind of children I was looking for." The doctor replied, "You're never going to have a life!" My friend responded ever so calmly, "This is my life."

"No one has greater love than this: that one should lay down his life for his friends." (John/ Yohanan 15:13)

The greatest love there is requires total *sacrifice.* You must lay down your life in order to live His life. You literally cannot do it without His heart. The prayer, "change my heart Yahweh" must become your daily supplication or else you'll never make it. This level of love is foreign to us. We must make it natural by daily slaying our natural tendencies and taking on Yahweh's characteristics. There will be a struggle, but you can walk in victory.

Defining what Father has specifically asked of you may take some time. When you discover it don't be surprised if you are struggling with the His plans for you. Committing your works to the Father will take much effort on your part, remember to relinquish your control of the situation and submit to Him.

# Chapter Four: Laying Aside Every Weight

"We too, then, having so great a cloud of witnesses all around us, let us lay aside every weight and the sin which so easily entangles us; and let us run with endurance the race set before us. Looking to the Princely Leader and Perfecter of our belief, Yahshua, who for the joy that was set before Him endured the stake, having despised the shame, and sat down at the right hand of the throne of Elohim. For consider Him who endured such opposition from sinners against Himself, lest you become weary and

---

faint in your lives. You have not yet resisted unto blood, striving against sin." (Hebrews / Ibrim 12:1-4)

What are your weights? Do you really know? Many of us state the obvious when it comes to things that easily lead us astray. Obesity, pornography, television, the list goes on. Let me pose a question to you. How many idols do you own? This is an often overlooked topic, yet is plagues the body of Messiah tremendously. Idols build pride, the more we acquire the better we think we are.
Leviticus 26 opens with an admonition.

"Do not make idols for yourselves, and do not set up a carved image or a pillar for yourselves and do not place a stone image in your land to bow down to it. For I am Yahweh your Elohim."

For the most part when we consider idols we visualize tall statues and small figurines. This is true. However, idolatry goes far and above this limited

---

definition. Let's see what the dictionary has to say.
"An image used as an object of worship. One that is
adored, often blindly, or excessively. Something visible but
without substance."

*Source: The American Heritage® Dictionary of the English Language,*
*Fourth Edition Copyright © 2000 by Houghton Mifflin Company.*
*All rights reserved.*

To excessively adore something is to idolize it. That
makes idolatry very personal and unique to each individual.
What I adore may not be what you consider admirable.
Seeing that idolatry is unique to each individual, then we
know that idolatry is also found in the heart. This is what
Yahweh had to say regarding this phenomenon.

"And some of the elders of Israel came to me and sat before
me; and the word of Yahweh came to me saying, "Son of
man, these men have set up idols in their hearts, and have
put the stumbling block of their crookedness before their
face. Should I let them inquire of Me at all?" (Ezekiel /

Yehezqel 14:2)

When I first read this my eyes lingered on that last sentence. It attacks relationship dead on. "Should I let them inquire of me at all?" With that statement, Yahweh is informs that He hesitates to communicate with us when we have idols in our hearts. Our prayers are directly hindered when we harbor idols.

What happens when we excessively adore something or someone other than Yahweh? Verse five of the same chapter states that we become estranged from Yahweh. In other words, we veer off the path and follow our idols instead of Yahweh.

"For anyone of the house of Israel, or of the strangers who sojourn in Israel who separates himself from Me, and sets up his idols in his heart and puts the stumbling block of crookedness before his face, and shall come to a prophet to inquire of him concerning Me, I Yahweh shall answer him Myself. And I shall set My face against that man and make him a sign and a proverb, and I shall cut him off from the midst of My people. And you shall know that I am Yahweh." (Ezekiel / Yehezqel 14:7-8)

In the time in which this was recorded Yahweh only spoke through the prophets. For Yahweh to state that when a man comes to a prophet concerning Himself that He will answer the offender personally is a huge deal. In addition to that, this personal confrontation is for the sole purpose of punishment and excommunication. That ought to strike fear into anyone.

What is in your heart eventually manifests itself in the natural. Your heart feeds your mind and your mind conceives the thought. That is why it is important to watch the gates of our eyes.

When we are drawn away, it is because of what was already in our heart, fed our mind, and our mind manifested the sin outwardly. This is why Yahshua said if a man looks upon a woman lustfully, that man has already committed adultery in his heart (Matthew 5:28). The heart is your source.

"Let no one say when he is enticed, "I am enticed by Elohim," for Elohim is not enticed by evil matters, and He entices no one. Each one is enticed when he is drawn away by his own desires and trapped. Then, when desire has conceived, it gives birth to sin. And sin, when it has been accomplished, brings forth death. Do not go astray my beloved brothers." (James / Ya'aqob) 1:13-15)

A good way to recognize deeply rooted idols in your heart is to look around you. According to James, whatever is in your heart will eventually manifest itself in the natural. That includes idols. Now for those who are breathing a sigh of relief and thinking "I'm glad I don't have any idols in my home!" Think again. Idolatry is not limited to our modern English understanding.

**Defining Idols**

Many people do not recognize the idols in their

lives. Let's start with collections. Are you an avid collector of dolls, stamps, teddy bears, movies, etc..? Consider how much money you've put out for these artifacts. Now think about how much money you would earn had you invested it properly instead of wasting it on "stuff". Or, better yet, how many hungry people could you have fed? What do you think is more important to our heavenly Father? What compels you to add to your collection? Why is your collection so important to you and what are some feelings you have regarding burning (not selling) these collections in the fire? Let's go back to Leviticus 26:1.

"Do not make idols for yourselves, and do not set up a carved image or a pillar for yourselves, and do not place a stone image in your land...."

I want to zero in on the word "make". It comes from the Hebrew word "asah". The word "asah" expands and explains what Yahweh meant when He said "Do not make (asah) for yourselves idols..." The word "asah" has multiple meanings. Let's review each one.


1. **to do, fashion, accomplish, produce**: This is very much like our English definition of make.

2. **To work, prepare, to make an offering:** Expands on the definition of make to include preparation. "Do not prepare idols for yourselves."

3. **To attend to, to put in order:** Expands to include organization. Do not give any attention to idols or even organize them (put on a shelf, organize within a cabinet, create a special place for them in your home.)

4. **To acquire or purchase:** Speaks for itself, do not even buy them.

5. **To appoint, ordain, or institute:** This definition ties into the third definition. To appoint, ordain, or institute means we are giving attention to the idol and putting it in a certain order. We do this with things and with people. For instance, pastors are often appointed and ordained, only to later be idolized.

6. **To observe or celebrate:** Do not celebrate idols or

---

observe their holiday. Makes you think about the secular calendar doesn't it?

7. **To bring about:** Do not cause an idol to be created.

8. **To use:** Don't use idols.

9. **To spend:** Don't spend money on idols.

10. **To press or squeeze:** This may sound a little strange at first until you consider that certain metals are fashioned by pressing and squeezing.

The reason why I chose to cover every definition of "make" or "asah" is because many people choose to focus in on the latter part of this verse "to bow down to it." With that they justify purchasing idols because they are not bowing down to it. However when you review the entire definition you know that an idol celebrated (such as during a holiday to honor it) will cause your heart (and maybe your knees too) to bow down. Your heart bows down when exorbitant quantities of money is spent to purchase idols (something that you have excessive admiration for). Your heart is bowed down if the very thought of losing your treasured possessions reduces you to tears.

"Hear O My People, and let me warn you, O Israel, if you would listen to Me! Let there be no strange mighty one among you, and do not bow down to a foreign mighty one. I am Yahweh, your Elohim." (Psalms / Tehillim 81:8-10)

**Destroying Idols**

Usually when you see the destruction of idols in Scripture, fire is involved. Idols shouldn't be transferred to another person. They should be destroyed beyond recognition.

**Refiner's Fire**

Of course, idolatry in the heart cannot simply be tossed into an open flame, with one exception. Yahweh's refining fire will destroy idols and purify our hearts, if we simply submit to His will.   Consider David's story.

King David was beloved of Yahweh and a worshiper at heart. He loved to worship. David fell into the sin of blood guiltiness on two levels, possibly three. Blood guiltiness is the result of several different sins. Consider the following Scriptures.

**Leviticus / Wayyiqra 17:1-7**

And Yahweh spoke to Mosheh, saying, "Speak to Aharon, to his sons, and to all the children of Yisra'el, and say to them, 'This is the word which Yahweh has commanded, saying, "Any man from the house of Yisra'el who slaughters a **bull or a lamb or a goat** in the camp, or who slaughters it outside the camp, and does not bring it to the door of the Tent of Meeting, to bring an offering to Yahweh before the Dwelling Place of Yahweh, blood-guilt is reckoned to that man. **He has shed blood, and that man shall be cut off from among his people**, in order that the children of Yisra'el bring their slaughterings which they slaughter in the open field. And they shall bring them to Yahweh at the door of the Tent of meeting, to the priest, and slaughter them as peace offerings to Yahweh. And the priest shall sprinkle the blood on the altar of Yahweh at the door of the Tent of Meeting, and shall burn the fat for a sweet fragrance to Yahweh. And let them no longer slaughter their slaughterings to demons, after whom they whored. This is a law forever for them throughout their generations.

Punishment for killing an animal consecrated for worship in sport is excommunication. This is an eternal law.

**Leviticus / Wayyiqra 20:9**

"For everyone who curses his father or mother shall certainly be put to death - he has cursed his father or his mother, his blood is on him."

The power of death and life is in the tongue (Proverbs 18:21), we can speak blessings or curses in a variety of ways. A spoken curse over your parents makes you guilty of shedding your own blood. It is equivalent to suicide.

"When a man has a wayward and rebellious son who is not listening to the voice of his father or the voice of his mother, and who, when they have disciplined him, does not listen to them, then his father and his mother shall take hold of him and bring him out to the elders of his city, to the gate of his city, and shall say to the elders of his city, 'This son of our is wayward and rebellious. He is not listening to our voice, he is a glutton and a drunkard.' Then all the men of the city shall stone him to death with stones. Thus you shall purge the evil from your midst. And let all Israel hear and fear." (Deuteronomy / Debarim 21:18-21)

Notice this is in direct connection to the promise attached to the 5th commandment: "Respect your father and your mother, **so that your days are prolonged** upon the soil which Yahweh your Elohim is giving you." (Exodus 20:12)

**Leviticus / Wayyiqra 20:11**

"And a man who lies with the wife of his father has uncovered the nakedness of his father, both of them shall certainly be put to death, their blood is upon him."

**Leviticus / Wayyiqra 20:12**

"And a man who lies with his daughter-in-law both of them shall certainly be put to death, they have made confusion, their blood is upon them."

**Leviticus / Wayyiqra 20:13**

"And a man who lies with a male as he lies with a woman; both of them have done an abomination, they shall certainly be put to death, their blood is upon them."

**Leviticus / Wayyiqra 20:16**

"And a woman who approaches any beast and mates with it: you shall kill the woman and the beast, they shall certainly be put to death, their blood is upon them."

**Leviticus / Wayyiqra 20:27**

"And a man or a woman in whom there is a medium, or who are spiritist shall certainly be put to death, they are to stone them with stones. Their blood is upon them."

### Summary of bloodguilt according to the law:
(There are more throughout Scripture)

1. Killing an animal consecrated for worship just for the fun of it.
2. Blaspheming the Spirit of Yahweh. (Eternal guilt is the result).

3. Disobedience to parents / speaking against parents.

4. Incest

5. Bestiality

6. Homosexuality

7. Witchcraft

8. Murder

Notice in these verses that as the punishment is executed, *the ones doing the stoning are free and clear of blood guiltiness.* Scripture repeatedly states that "their blood is upon them," meaning the one who transgressed the law is also guilty of causing their own blood to be shed even though someone else threw the stones. To make yourself blood-guilty is equivalent to committing suicide.

Yahweh MUST receive recompense for our shed blood. Here is Yahweh's admonishment to Noah after the ark settled on dry land.

"But only your blood for your lives I require, from the hand of every beast I require it, and from the hand of man. From the hand of every man's brother I require the life of man. Whoever sheds man's blood, by man his blood is shed, for in the image of Elohim has He made man. As for you, bear fruit and increase, bring forth teemingly in the earth and increase in it." (Genesis / Bereshith 9:5-7)

Here is what Yahshua said in Luke 11:49-51. "And because of this the Wisdom of Elohim said, 'I shall send them prophets and emissaries, and some of them they shall kill and persecute,' so that the blood of all the prophets which was shed from the foundation of the world shall be required of this generation, from the blood of Abel to the blood of Zekaryah who perished between the altar and the Dwelling Place. Yea, I say to you, it shall be required of this generation."

In Second Samuel chapter eleven, we read about King David's grave error and the affect it had on his life. During the time when all kings were at war, David was at home. Outside he saw Bathsheba, his neighbor's wife bathing on the rooftop. Bathsheba had just finished her menstrual cycle and was completing her monthly purification. David sent for her, engaged in relations with her, and she became pregnant. According to the law, both of them should be stoned to death and their blood be upon them.

David initially tried to cover his mistake by sending for Bathsheba's husband, Uryah, in hopes that he would lie with his wife. If so, they could pass the baby off as his. He instructed Uriyah to go down to his house and wash his feet. (2 Samuel 11:8) Uriyah was a good man and didn't think it was fitting that he went home to enjoy his wife, while every other man was at war.

When David saw that he couldn't get Uriyah to go home to his wife he arranged to have him murdered. His plan worked, and Uriyah died on the battlefield along with some of David's servants. David had made himself blood-guilty again. After the appropriate period of mourning for Bathsheba, she married David and bore him a son. Yahweh was furious with what David had done and vowed to punish him openly for what he did in secret. In addition to that, there was still the dilemma of the child.

Yahweh had tremendous mercy upon both David and Bathsheba, but that mercy was not without consequence. Yahweh sent Nathan the prophet to David to deliver the following prophecy.

"Why have you despised the Word of Yahweh to do evil in His eyes? You have killed Uriyah the Hittite with the sword, and his wife you took to be your wife and you have killed him with the sword of the children of Ammon. And now, the sword does not turn aside from your house because you have despised Me, and have taken the wife of Uriyah the Hittite to be your wife." Thus said Yahweh, "See I am raising up evil against you from your own house and shall take your wives before your eyes and give them to your neighbor, and he shall lie with your wives in the sight of this sun. For you did it in secret, but I shall do this deed before all Yisrael, and before the sun." (2 Samuel 12:9-12)

David struggled with the pride of life, after all Yahweh had done for him, after all he accomplished, it wasn't enough. He wanted more. Yahweh said to him "I anointed you king over Israel, and I delivered you from the hand of Shaul, and I gave you your master's house and your master's wives into your bosom, and gave you the house of Yisrael and Yehudah. *And if that were not enough, I also would have given you much more!*" (2 Samuel 12:7-8)

Immediately after Nathan delivered the message from Yahweh, the child fell ill and David fasted and spent all night lying on the ground. Somewhere around this time, David penned Psalm 51, which was written for the public song service (not private prayer).

~~~~~~~~~~~~~~~~~~~~~~~~~~~~~~~~~~~~~~~~~~~~~~~~

## Psalm 51 (KJV)

1 Have mercy upon me, O Yahweh, according to thy lovingkindness: according unto the multitude of thy tender mercies, blot out my transgressions.

---

[2] Wash me thoroughly from mine iniquity, and cleanse me from my sin.

[3] For I acknowledge my transgressions: and my sin is ever before me.

[4] Against thee, thee only, have I sinned, and done this evil in thy sight: that thou mightest be justified when thou speakest, and be clear when thou judgest.

[5] Behold, I was shapen in iniquity; and in sin did my mother conceive me.

[6] Behold, thou desirest truth in the inward parts: and in the hidden part thou shalt make me to know wisdom.

[7] Purge me with hyssop, and I shall be clean: wash me, and I shall be whiter than snow.

[8] Make me to hear joy and gladness; that the bones which thou hast broken may rejoice.

[9] Hide thy face from my sins, and blot out all mine iniquities.

[10] Create in me a clean heart, O Yahweh; and renew a right spirit within me.

[11] Cast me not away from thy presence; and take not

thy holy spirit from me.

<sup>12</sup> Restore unto me the joy of thy salvation; and uphold me with thy free spirit.

<sup>13</sup> Then will I teach transgressors thy ways; and sinners shall be converted unto thee.

<sup>14</sup> Deliver me from bloodguiltiness, O Yahweh, thou El of my salvation: and my tongue shall sing aloud of thy righteousness.

<sup>15</sup> O Yahweh, open thou my lips; and my mouth shall shew forth thy praise.

<sup>16</sup> For thou desirest not sacrifice; else would I give it: thou delightest not in burnt offering.

<sup>17</sup> The sacrifices of Yahweh are a broken spirit: a broken and a contrite heart, O God, thou wilt not despise.

<sup>18</sup> Do good in thy good pleasure unto Zion: build thou the walls of Jerusalem.

<sup>19</sup> Then shalt thou be pleased with the sacrifices of righteousness, with burnt offering and whole burnt offering: then shall they offer bullocks upon thine altar.

On the seventh day, the child died. His servants were scared to tell him that his son had died because he was in such great mourning. David perceived that the child had died and they relented and confessed that his son was gone. After that, David had one of the strangest reactions to a child dying ever recorded. He got up, washed and anointed himself, changed his clothes and went into the house of Yahweh to worship! After that, he went home and got something to eat. Even his servants didn't understand why his reaction for it was one of *celebration and joy.* Let's see why.

David fathered a child through an adulterous affair. That would make the child a illegitimate according to the law.

Deuteronomy 23:1-2. "No one wounded, crushed or whose member is cut off does enter the assembly of Yahweh. No one of illegitimate birth does enter the assembly of Yahweh, even a tenth generation of his does not enter the assembly of Yahweh."

If David's son had lived, he would have been a witness against his father. His illegitimate son would have been a testament that David and his descendants are cut off from the assembly of Yahweh, up to the tenth generation. (In modern day terms - he was excommunicated or shunned from the assembly, or Sabbath meeting for 10 generations).

The last illegitimate birth through this line was a result of Judah's transgression with Tamar, which resulted in twins Pharez and Zerah. (Genesis 38)

According to the genealogy recorded in the first chapter of Matthew, David was the tenth generation after the transgression; the generation that would *finally* be allowed to enter in the assembly of Yahweh.

**(Matthew 1:3-6)**

And Judas begat
Phares and Zera of Thamar;
Generation 1 (illegit. birth)

and Phares begat Esrom;

Generation 2

and Esrom begat Aram;

Generation 3

And Aram begat Aminadab;

Generation 4

and Aminadab begat Naasson;

Generation 5

and Naasson begat Salmon;

Generation 6

And Salmon begat Boaz

of Rachab;

Generation 7

and Boaz begat Obed of Ruth;

Generation 8

and Obed begat Jesse;

Generation 9

And Jesse begat

David the king;

Generation 10

When Yahweh put away David's sin by allowing the illegitimate child to die, this meant that he and his children after him did not have to be shunned from the assembly for the next 10 generations. The transgression was blotted out! Soon afterwards, David wrote Psalm 122:1.

**"I was glad when they said unto me, let us go into the house of Yahweh."**

The word "glad" is translated from the word "samach" which means "to arrogantly rejoice." David was arrogantly rejoicing over what the Father had done for Him! He refused to look at the single child who died because of his sin, but rather he arrogantly rejoiced over TEN GENERATIONS of his seed that would LIVE as a result of Yahweh's mercy. He was glad to go into the house of Yahweh because for the past 10 generations his lineage was shunned as a result of sin, then he fell over the same stumbling block and committed the SAME SIN and would have been further shunned for an additional 10 years. A twenty generation sentence of **not being allowed** to worship was cut in half by the Father's mercy.

Even still, David's idolatry and pride had severe consequences, his son Amnon, raped his sister Tamar. As a result, his brother Absalom hated him. Two years passed and Absalom murdered Amnon in revenge. Absalom fled for three years and David mourned his departure. Later, David was grieved again when his Absalom was killed. Yahweh exacted His revenge, and David was punished.

Even though the punishment was severe, it was far less than what he should have suffered according to the law.

There is a connection between putting away (destroying) all your idols and receiving great blessing from the Father.

"Cast away from you all the transgressions by which you have transgressed, and make for yourselves a new heart and a new spirit. For why should you die, O house of Yisrael? For I have no pleasure in the death of one who dies." declares the Master Yahweh. "So turn back and live!" (Ezekiel 18:31-32)

If you are brave enough and committed to the Father, turning away from idolatry is sure to bring life to your body and spirit.

# Chapter Five: Self-Esteem

"Not to us O Yahweh, not to us, but to Your Name give esteem, for your kindness, for your truth." (Psalm / Tehillim 115:1)

The dictionary definition of self-esteem is, "a realistic respect or favorable impression of oneself," or an exaggeratedly favorable impression of oneself." There was only one synonym listed; pride. Pride and self-esteem share the same definition, however society pushes us to cherish and cultivate self-esteem as if it is necessary for our survival. It isn't. In fact, it hinders our walk with the

Father. We should have esteem in Him. When we give Yahweh esteem, we automatically feel great about who we are because we are His children. Self –esteem, without the Creator of all life, is merely a fanciful name for pride. We have to learn, like the psalmist, to give esteem to His name alone, and recognize that without Him we can do nothing.

"I have strength to do all through Messiah who empowers me." (Philippians 4:13)

Yahshua Messiah must be the source of our strength in all that we do. To believe that the source of strength lies in our own power is deceptive.

First Corinthians 13 says, "If I speak with the tongues of men and of messengers, but do not have love, I have become as sounding brass or a clanging cymbal. And if I have prophecy, and know all secrets and all knowledge, and if I have all belief, so as to remove mountains, but do not have love, I am none at all. And if I give out all my possessions to feed the poor, and if I give my body to be burned but do not have love I am not profited at all." (1 Corinthians 13:1-3)

Whatever we do, our focus needs to point to Yahweh, our Heavenly Father.

"And when Yahshua was in Beth Anyah at the house of Shimon the leper, a woman came to Him having an alabaster flask of costly perfume and she poured it on His head as He sat at the table. And when His taught ones saw it, they were much displeased saying, "To what purpose is this waste? For this perfume could have been sold for much and given to the poor."

However when Yahshua noticed it, He said to them, "Why do you trouble woman? For she has done a good work toward Me. For you always have the poor with you, but Me you do not have always. For in pouring this perfume on My body, she did it for My burial. Truly I say to you wherever this Good News is proclaimed in all the world, what this woman has done shall be spoken of also to her remembrance." (Matthew 26:6-13)

We must constantly re-evaluate whether or not we are laying our lives down for Yahweh's glory. Allow Yahweh to reveal what it really means to worship Him rather than *worshiping ourselves through Him.*

Self-esteem is a curious thing. It can be given and taken away by other people. I know of a young girl who is plagued by an extremely low self-esteem. She knows Yahweh and believes what His Word says about who she is, yet she is consistently bombarded with negative remarks on a daily basis. One evening a positive comment came her way, and I could literally feel the hush in the spirit. Demons were silenced and confused, on the basis of one positive comment. Truly life and death is in the power of the tongue. We can share Yahweh's esteem and love with others or break down one another with our words. The tongue is a sharp sword and if not used carefully, can yield many years of pain.

I am thankful that I was able to witness the turn-around for this child, and I pray that she has many more words of encouragement coming her way.

### Humility vs. Low Self-Esteem

"Pride comes, then comes shame; but with the humble is wisdom" (Psalms 11:2)

"If then, there is any encouragement in Messiah, if any comfort of love, if any fellowship of Spirit if any affection and compassion, make my joy complete by being of the same mind, having the same love, one in being and of purpose, doing none at all through selfishness or self-conceit, but in humility consider others better than yourselves." (Philippians 2:1-3)

How do you get to the point of true humility without tumbling over into the area of low self-esteem? Humility is defined as having a *modest* opinion of one's own worth and importance. This is a healthy dose of esteem. However, people suffering from low self-esteem do not regard themselves at all. This is an insult to our Creator, who created us in His image and likeness. If we consider ourselves worthless, what are we saying about Him?

Scripture defines a person who has a modest opinion of him or herself as wise. A humble person is identified by their spiritual fruit.

"Who is wise and understanding among you? Let him show by his good behavior his works in meekness of wisdom." (James 3:13)

"In the same way, you younger ones be subject to elders. Gird yourselves with humility toward one another, for Elohim resists the proud, but gives favor to the humble. Humble yourselves then, under the mighty hand of Elohim so that He exalts you in due time, casting all your worry upon Him for he is concerned about you." (1 Peter 5:5-7)

True humility is not low self-esteem. True humility is confidence carefully placed in the Father, and with that placement, there is wisdom.

Scripture also warns us of false humility.

"Let no one deprive you of the prize, one who takes delight in false humility and worship of messengers, taking his stand on what he has not seen, puffed up by his fleshly mind, and not holding fast to the Head, from whom all the Body nourished and knit together by joints and ligaments grows with the growth of Elohim." (Colossians 2:17-19)

False humility finds its source in outward regulations without relationship.

"If then, you died with Messiah from the elementary matters of the world why as though living in the world do you subject yourselves to regulations: "Do not touch, do not taste, do not handle," - which are all to perish with use according to the **commands and teachings of men?** These indeed have an appearance of wisdom in self-imposed worship, humiliation and harsh treatment of the body of no value at all, only for the satisfaction of the flesh. (Colossians 2:20-23)

The above passage is sometimes used to validate lawlessness, a disregard of Torah. However, if we look at the above passage without blinders or outside influences we can very clearly see that Father is strictly referring to the commandments that **men** added to His Word. He is not referring to the commandments that He spoke forth out of His own mouth.

Following the teachings of men, above the Word of Yahweh, is a marker for false humility, folly, and self-destruction.

# *Part Two*

# Pride

# Chapter Six: Overcoming the Ultimate Stumbling Block

"Before destruction comes pride, and before a fall a haughty spirit!" (Proverbs 16:18)

We've already seen what Joseph's pride cost him. He suffered a mighty fall. However, he survived. That is what I want to focus in on - survival. It is possible to walk through the muck of destruction, and the fall, after experiencing a tremendous blow to your pride. What you do afterward can make you or break you, and it is very important.

---

I met a homeless man in a post office once. It came about by curious circumstances. I was at home, knowing that I needed to mail out a letter that same day. The post office closed early being that it was Sunday and I had very little time to get there. Thankfully, the post office was about a mile away from my home. While gathering my things and preparing to leave I sensed that Yahweh wanted me to hurry and that he had something for me waiting at the post office. Of course, I thought I had some wonderful surprise in my mailbox. I didn't. What I did get was a "chance" encounter with a homeless man. He was dirty and smelly and carried some of his belongings with him in small shopping bag. The rest of his belongings, he told me, was in a shopping cart hidden away under a bridge.

At the time, I was involved with an organization dedicated to rehabilitating the homeless through shelter, food, and job programs. I gave him the information and counted on him to call and get down there by train. The train ticket would only cost him $1.20 and he had shared with me that he gets a $675 social security check each month.

The next week I went down to the post office at the same time, and there he was standing by the heater. It was snowing outside and very cold. I was concerned. He proceeded to show me his frost bitten hands and knees. He also told me where he slept in the evenings, and that he was sheltered from the storm, even though he was outside.

I asked him again about going to seek help. He wrote down his contact information in case I needed to get a hold of him. He was good friends with the man who owned the local shoe store. He informed me that I could contact the shoe store; they would know where to find him. When he wrote down his name, I looked up at him curiously. His name was preceded by many titles; two of which were Reverend Dr. He began to explain starting with extending his hand.

"Shake my hand," he said. I did. "You've just shaken the hand that has shaken the hand of Dr. Martin Luther King Jr. and Jesse Jackson." He went on an on with a long list of famous names. He told me about how he enjoyed dinners with Dr. Martin Luther King Jr. during his time as a professional photographer. I stayed for a while and listened to his fascinating stories. I was transported back forty years to the life he had as a young man. Not once did he mention how he became homeless. I did hear about all the people he met, and why his name required so many titles.

When I looked outside and saw the snow piling up I offered to pay for a hotel room so he could spend the evening inside, sheltered from the soon-coming snowstorm. He refused; telling me that he had to get his shopping cart with all his belongings by 6 am, and that there was no way he'd get there in time. "I'd oversleep," he said.

Week after week for the next two months, I went to the post office and chatted with him. I looked past the smell, dirt and grime, and running sores. There was a person underneath it all; and that person needed help emotionally more than he did physically. I also understood that my homeless friend thought Yahweh had forgotten him. It was really He who forgot Yahweh. He chose to dwell on his past and puff himself up with importance by using fancy titles before his name. Even after the fall and destruction, he chose to serve pride rather than the Father and that is why he never really pursued help. If he did get help, he would have to live in the real world and the real world would eventually hold him before a mirror and show him what he looks like now.

When I moved out of state I lost touch with him but I'm sure he's still in that small town eating stale ice cream out of the garbage, and fighting with the squirrels for food. He never sought help, even though it was freely offered. Whoever befriends him is sure to get a book of stories on how great he used to be - forty years ago.

In this battle we have choices. We can choose to overshadow our faults or face them and move on. When we face our faults and use that in a positive light, so many people will be blessed and encouraged by our testimony. Our testimonies are positive weapons and should not be overlooked. People feel better by simply knowing that others have walked the same road and failed, but later succeeded when they chose to get back up and fight.

# Chapter Seven: That Which Yahweh Hates

"These six matters Yahweh hates, and seven are an abomination to Him: A proud look, a lying tongue, and hands shedding innocent blood, a heart devising wicked schemes, feet quick to run to evil, a false witness breathing out lies, and one who causes strife among the brothers. My son, watch over your father's command, and do not forsake the Torah of your mother." (Proverbs 6:16-20)

Hate is a very strong word. It leaves no room for redemption. To hate is to bring finality. It is very rare for that which is hated, to later be loved. Yahweh declares in His Word that there are six matters that He absolutely hates. The first on the list is a proud look. The word look in that passage literally translates to "eye." Yahweh carefully weighs how we view others. You don't have to say a word in order to fall victim to this sin.

Throughout Scripture Yahweh is passionate regarding this issue.

"A haughty look, a proud heart, the lamp of the wrong, are sin." (Proverbs 21:4)

"Him who secretly slanders his neighbor I cut off. I do not tolerate one who has a haughty look and a proud heart." (Psalm 101:5)

Pride cannot exist very long in the heart of a true

believer because Yahweh is diligently fighting against it. A humiliating (and most likely public) fall and destruction is the promise to those who harbor pride within their hearts.

*Part Three*

# Sanctification

# Chapter Eight: A Portrait of Purity

"But you are a chosen race, a royal priesthood, a set apart nation, a people for a possession, that you should proclaim the praises of Him who called you out of darkness into His marvelous light, who once were not a people, but now the people of Elohim; who had not obtained compassion, but now obtained compassion." (1 Peter 2:9-10)

We are called to separate ourselves from darkness, to be in the world but not of it, and keep ourselves pure before the Father. This is a tall order considering we're bombarded with paganism on a day-to-day basis. For example, the names of our months and days of the week are named after pagan gods. Certain planets in our Solar System have been dedicated and named after idols. In a pure heart, there is no place for pride. Yahweh gives the great reward of being able to stand in the most set apart place to those with pure hearts.

"Who does go up into the mountain of Yahweh? And who does stand in His set apart place? He who has clean hands and a clean heart, who did not bring his life to naught, and did not swear deceivingly. He receives a blessing from Yahweh and righteousness from the Elohim of his deliverance." (Psalm 24:43-5)

How can Israel remain a portrait of purity in a world gone corrupt?

**Worldly Purity**: The world's standard of purity doesn't

exist. We live in a day and age where anything goes. Purity by definition means "freedom from contamination, pollution, or mixture." With regard to the world, it is a stinking cesspool and we would do well to separate ourselves from it.

**Biblical Purity:** We see in the Old Covenant, strict standards for keeping purity throughout Israel's encampment. Throughout the book of Leviticus we are reminded of the responsibility of being a royal nation set apart for the Father. There were guidelines to follow for ceremonial worship and guidelines for everyday living. Everything from the food they ate to marital relations were covered. If Israel broke these regulations many times they either died or had to be excommunicated.

In order to prepare Israel to receive Yahshua Messiah as Savior, there had to be a standard for purity.

"Therefore, the Torah became our trainer unto Messiah, in order to be declared right by belief. And after

belief has come, we are no longer under a trainer."
(Galatians 3:24-25)

Although the majority of these regulations still stand today, keeping them is not what justifies us before Yahweh. Faith in His Son is what purifies and justifies us before the Father. It is through this relationship we can put away pride and walk in purity.

Why keep the instructions regarding separation, or any instruction for that matter, if it doesn't justify us before the Father? Simply put, we are called to grow up in Torah and not remain in one place.

"Therefore having left the word of the beginning of the Messiah, let us go on to perfection, not laying again the foundation of repentance from dead works, and of belief toward Elohim." (Hebrews 6:1)

If obedience to Torah led Israel closer to Yahshua yesterday, it certainly will do the same thing today. For He is the same yesterday, today, and forever. Therefore, He Himself has warned us.

"Do not think that I came to destroy the Torah or the Prophets. I did not come to destroy but to complete. For truly I say to you, till the heaven and the earth shall pass away, one jot or title shall by no means pass from the Torah till all be done. Whoever then breaks one of the least of these commands, and teaches men so, shall be called the least in the reign of the heavens: but whoever does and teaches them, he shall be called great in the reign of the heavens." (Matthew 5:17-18)

Obedience to Torah without Messiah is incomplete; you must have both. Obedience without compromise brings you closer and closer to Yahshua Messiah and the love of the Father.

"If you love me, you shall guard My commands. And I shall ask the Father, and He shall give you another Helper to stay with you forever, the Spirit of Truth whom the world is unable to receive because it does not see Him or know Him. But you know Him for He stays with you and shall be in you." (John 14:15-17)

"As the Father has loved Me, I also loved you. Stay in My love. If you guard My commands, you shall stay in My love, even as I have guarded My Father's commands and stay in His love. These words I have spoken to you so that My joy might be in you and that you joy might be complete." (John 15:10-11)

"And He said to him, "Why do you call Me good? No one is good except One - Elohim. But if you wish to enter into life, guard the commands." (Matthew 19:17)

"Blessed are those doing His commands, so that the authority shall be theirs unto the tree of life and to enter through the gates into the city. But outside are the dogs and those who enchant with drugs and those who whore and the murderers, and the idolaters and all who love to do falsehood." (Revelation 22:14-15)

# Chapter Nine: The Robe of Righteousness

"I greatly rejoice in Yahweh, my being exults in my Elohim. For He has put garments of deliverance on me. He has covered me with the robe of righteousness as a bridegroom decks himself with ornaments and as a bride adorns herself with her jewels." (Isaiah 61:10)

It is interesting to note that one of the garments of deliverance is the garment of righteousness. Deliverance

---

indicates freedom from a certain oppression. It is safe to conclude that because pride is an oppression resulting in bondage, one of the spiritual garments we need in order for deliverance to occur is the garment of righteousness. Righteousness is defined as right living before Yahweh. We are commanded to be clothed with righteousness.

"Let your priests put on righteousness and your kind ones shout for joy." (Psalm 132:9)

 It cannot be achieved on our own, or through man invented rules and regulations. It has to occur through the Spirit of Yahweh and the Truth of His Word (both His spoken Word and His written Word). These things draw us closer to Him. It has the opposite effect of unrighteousness, which pushes us further away.

### Isaiah 59
"Look, the hand of Yahweh has not become too short to save, nor His hear too heavy to hear.

But your crookedness have separated you from your Elohim. And your sins have hidden His face from you.

For your hands have been defiled with blood and your fingers with crookedness; your lips have spoken falsehood, your tongue mutters unrighteousness.

No one calls for righteousness, and no one pleads for the truth. They trust in emptiness and speak worthlessness; they conceive trouble and bring forth wickedness.

They have hatched adders' eggs and they weave the spider's web. Whoever eats their eggs dies, and when one is broken, an adder is hatched.

Their webs do not become garments, nor do they cover themselves with their works. Their works are works of wickedness and a deed of violence is in their hands. Their feet run to evil and they hurry to shed innocent blood. Their thoughts are thoughts of wickedness; wasting and ruin are in their highways.

The way of peace, they have not known and there is no right ruling in their ways. They have made crooked paths for themselves; whoever treads in them shall not know peace. Therefore, right ruling has been far from us, and righteousness does not reach us. We look for light but there is darkness for brightness, but we walk in thick darkness!

We feel for the wall like the blind and we feel as without eyes. At noon we stumble as at twilight, in deserted places, like the dead.

All of us growl like bears and moan sadly like doves. We look for right ruling but there is none; for deliverance but it is far from us.

For our transgressions have increased before You, and our sins witnessed against us. For our transgressions are with us, and as for our crookedness, we know them; transgressing, and being untrue to Yahweh, and turning away from our Elohim speaking oppression and apostasy, conceiving and pondering words of falsehood from the heart.

And right ruling is driven back, and righteousness stands far off. For the truth has fallen in the street and right is unable to enter.

And the truth is lacking and whoever turns away from evil makes himself a prey. And Yahweh saw and it displeased Him that there was no right ruling.

And He saw that there was no man and was astonished that there was no intercessor. So His own arm saved for Him and His righteousness upheld him.

And He put on righteousness as a breastplate and a helmet of deliverance on His head. And He put on garments of vengeance for clothing, and wrapped Himself with ardour as a mantle.

According to their deeds, so He repays, wrath to His adversaries, recompense to His enemies. He repays recompense to the coastlands.

And they shall fear the Name of Yahweh from the west and His esteem from the rising of the sun, when He comes like a distressing stream which the Spirit of Yahweh drives on.

And the Redeemer shall come to Tsiyon (Zion) and to those turning from transgression in Yaaqob (Jacob), declares Yahweh. As for Me this is My covenant with them, said Yahweh. 'My Spirit that is upon you and My Words that I have put in your mouth, shall not be withdrawn from your mouth nor from the mouth your descendants, nor from the mouth of your descendants' descendants,' said Yahweh, 'from this time and forever.'"

After our initial salvation experience we must commit to sanctification beginning with the robe of righteousness which allows us to walk upright before the Father. Without it, evil, unrest, and judgement is the result.

Sanctification is a commitment to purity and as with all spiritual matters, we must make a choice. We can choose to go all the way without compromise and not get hung up on satan's stumbling blocks, or we can choose the world's way of mixture and compromise. The pride of life, although appealing in the beginning, will cost you much more than you are willing to pay.

"For the rest, my brothers, be strong in the Master and in the mightiness of His strength. Put on the complete armor of Elohim, for you to have power to stand against the schemes of the devil. Because we do not wrestle against flesh and blood, but against principalities, against authorities, against the world rulers of the darkness of this age, against spiritual matters of wickedness in the heavenlies.

Because of this, take up the complete armor of Elohim so that you have power to withstand in the evil day and having done all, to stand.

Stand, then, having girded your waist with truth, and having put on the breastplate of righteousness, and having fitted your feet with the preparation of the Good News of peace; above all having taken up the shield of belief which you shall have power to quench all the burning arrows of the wicked one.

Take also the helmet of deliverance and the sword of the Spirit which is the Word of Elohim, praying at all times, with all prayer and supplication in the Spirit, watching in all perseverance and supplication for all the set apart ones; also for me that a word might be given to me in the opening of my mouth to be bold in making known the secret of the Good News..." (Ephesians 6:10-19)

## Other Books by Sonya T. Anderson

Available at www.Amazon.com, www.LuLu.com, or
www.SonyaTAnderson.com

www.ingramcontent.com/pod-product-compliance
Lightning Source LLC
Chambersburg PA
CBHW051846040426
42447CB00006B/720